COLLECTING DUST

COLLECTING DUST

SONNETS
(THUS FAR)

Ronald E. Wheeler

Introduction by Jon A. Weatherly

RESOURCE *Publications* • Eugene, Oregon

COLLECTING DUST
Sonnets (Thus Far)

Copyright © 2021 Ronald E. Wheeler. All rights reserved. Except for brief quotations in critical publications or reviews, no part of this book may be reproduced in any manner without prior written permission from the publisher. Write: Permissions, Wipf and Stock Publishers, 199 W. 8th Ave., Suite 3, Eugene, OR 97401.

Resource Publications
An Imprint of Wipf and Stock Publishers
199 W. 8th Ave., Suite 3
Eugene, OR 97401

www.wipfandstock.com

PAPERBACK ISBN: 978-1-7252-9903-0
HARDCOVER ISBN: 978-1-7252-9904-7
EBOOK ISBN: 978-1-7252-9905-4

04/28/21

"No man is an island," John Donne asserts, and I would attest least of all poets. The poetic enterprise needs a response to complete its purpose of translating and transferring the human experience.

Therefore, I dedicate this volume to the myriad family, friends, colleagues, coworkers, fellow disciples, and, from time to time, strangers upon whom I have inflicted the readings of these sonnets.

Of special note, my thanks to:

Martha
for the time it took me away from you;

Marie
for the encouragement and copyediting expertise;

Jon
for the incentive and editorial guidance graciously given.

CONTENTS

Preface | xi
Introduction | xiii

Clothes Hamper for Time After Time

Blessing | 3
The Stretch | 4
Good Friday | 5
Meanwhile | 6
The Flying Crucifix | 7
Halloween | 8
Polaris | 9
Testimony | 10
Reflected Glory | 11
Greensleeves | 12
Thanksgiving | 13
Those Times | 14

Storage Tubs for Christ's Mass

A Celebrant's Prayer | 17
Waiting for Christmas | 18
To Open Gifts | 19

House of Bread | 20
Grace for Christmas Eve | 21
A Gathering of Fowls | 22
Cathedral Eve | 23
First Sunday | 24
Second Sunday | 25
Third Sunday | 26
Fourth Sunday | 27
Carol | 28

Table Crumbs for Friends and Lovers

Color Line | 31
Yokefellow | 32
Cade's Cove '97 | 33
Around the World | 34
Departure | 35
In Praise of Knowledge, Enthusiasm, and Engagement | 36
Love Kindled | 37
Your Heart or Mine? | 38
The Birds, The Bees, The Moon | 39
Candle Lighting | 40
Hope | 41
Love's Long Shadow | 42

Plot Numbers for Madison Cemeteries: Grave Stories

Headstones | 45
Madison Cemeteries | 46
Jason Ritter Crosley | 47
Connor Adler Carr | 48
Butler | 49

Walter Sands | 50
Matilda A. Sands | 51
Malinda P. Cort | 52
D. S. | 53
L. R. | 54
Bass | 55
Gerod Telek, Jr. | 56
Illegible Inscription | 57
Notes on the Cemeteries | 58

PREFACE

My inner instructor feels some consternation in putting these poems forward without an appendix, something like:

"How to Read the Sonnet," or

"A Survey of Sonnet Forms," or

"Read Others, Write Your Own: Sonnet Interpretation and Construction."

My editor, copy editor, and long-standing readers assure me that such attachments prove singularly unnecessary, if not downright distracting. Still, I cannot pass this occasion without stating a word or two about my fondness of this poetic fixed form.

I grew up in a household that valued reading and valued words placed in the air. Both my mother and father read to me. To this day I would as soon *hear* a book as read it. The children's poetry that my parents gave me employed bold rhythms and rhymes—particularly the poems of Eugene Field, James Whitcomb Riley, and Edgar Allan Poe. My father had his own repertoire of doggerel and ditties, some of which I still quote on occasion.

Although I came late to writing sonnets, I have long enjoyed the musicality of the form. I love lyric that sings. Petrarch, Chaucer, Shakespeare, and Spenser introduced me to the foundation and form of the sonnet. The Psalms, Dickinson, Frost, Eliot, and Stevens pushed me in rhetorical diction, imagery, and metaphor. Lennon & McCartney, Joni Mitchell, Paul Simon, Bob Dylan, James Taylor, Gordon Lightfoot, and Steve Taylor demonstrated how good storytelling marries sound and sense in ways that feel both conversational and dazzling.

Conversational and dazzling—I fail more often than succeed at those qualities, yet they point me to the sonnet. I hope you find one or two of these pieces that meet my aspiration and that fulfill yours.

Ronald E. Wheeler
Professor of English
Johnson University
January 2021

INTRODUCTION

I love the poems in this collection.

I love them for their attention to form. Art that stretches or even abandons form challenges its audience and extends the boundaries of the art. But classic forms are classic for good reason, their inexhaustible potential inviting new generations of artists. These poems honor the elegant tradition of the sonnet.

I love them for their sound. Just as it seemed the modern world had abandoned reading aloud and so forgotten that written words are supposed to make sounds, audio books have reminded us that words can make music. Poets, of course, or at least most of them, have never forsaken reading aloud. This poet, blessed with a keen ear and a rich voice, makes music at every opportunity. You can hear that voice reading these poems by streaming the audio at https://johnsonu.edu/WheelerPoems.

I love them because I connect through them to the humanity of the writer and of his subjects. They observe around and within. They draw me into their scenes and senses. They tell me about myself as they tell me about others.

I love them because they repeatedly express with honesty the paradox of Christian faith. If we may compare the Beatitudes, they speak from the condition of the faithful—need, alienation, longing—and to the expectant hope for a divine answer.

I love them for their blend of opacity and clarity. Poetry is supposed to challenge its reader, and these poems do. But to be more than a formal exercise, poetry must communicate. And these poems do, in ways that can engage even those who do not often read poetry.

Certainly, I know them and love them because I know and love their author. Ronald Wheeler has been my colleague for some seven years as I write. He has a welcome habit of walking down the office hallway to share his latest creation, first reading aloud, then providing printed copy. Having enjoyed every one of those premieres, I followed an impulse one day and promised him I would help as I could when he was ready to bring his poems to print, even though I have no formal qualifications to do so.

And so here we are. My colleague, friend, and brother has shared his art, and I was witness to that sharing.

Jon Weatherly
Professor of New Testament
Johnson University
January 2021

Clothes Hamper for
Time After Time

BLESSING

We welcome You, O sovereign God, to set
Our daily path both straight and clear—to make
A level road for weary feet to take—
A walk without reproach, without regret.

We seek a transformed mind and heart; we pray
To bend our winding wills to Your great good—
To do what we know, to be what we should—
By leaning on Your outstretched arm each day.

We sense how much You gave, how much you give—
A Treasure bound in terra clay; but greed
Inflames to have and hoard beyond our need,
Impoverishes the Way by which to live.

Our Father, we would bleed what we believe:
"It is more blessèd to give than receive."

Romans 12:2; Acts 20:35

THE STRETCH

We did not fall, except to fail His faith.
Instead of trust, we stretched the hand to clasp
What we refused to understand—belief
Betrayed seeds every garden's ground with grief.

Diminished by that choice, we still retain
Capacity, if not facility,
And just enough to open clenching fists
Where thorns and thistles sting with sweat and pain.

Our Maker gives, and we receive the gift,
No matter how impossible to hold.
But hold we must, until our loss from rain
And rust has turned us once again to trust.

So what can wash away this smudge of sod
From grasping? Nothing—but the blood of God.

Genesis 3:22; Philippians 2:5–7

GOOD FRIDAY

We call this Friday *good*, but where's the good
In death? And such a death—horrific, dark,
And lonely; a suffocating death—stark
Like barren trees with streaks of blackened wood.

Yet Good takes preparation, working through
A life prepared, a life in tune with Joy
Obedient—the homeward-absent boy
About his Father's house, the wise and true.

And Good takes time—in years of worship, days
Of prayer—to nurture words for hope and peace,
To comfort hearts, to ease the clinging grief
Of souls who stretch their hands for selfish ways.

For even though we live by seize and shove,
This Friday makes an open show of Love.

Romans 5:8

MEANWHILE

When sitting for the doctor's slow delay,
Recall the decades spent with Reuel.
When standing in the grocery line, replay
How thirty years at Nazareth avail.
When tapping fingers at the light's array,
Remember Saul upon his desert trail.
When passing moments turn to lasting days,
Reflect on Jonah's sign and death's dark veil.

If chafing, crushing time tic-tocs away,
Slow down, stay here, transcend the clock and pray.
Embrace the moment's solitude. You may
Invoke the Spirit's patience to prevail
If chafing, crushing time tic-tocs away.
Slow down, stay here, transcend the clock and pray.

Reuel pronounced: reh´ ü āl´

Seasoned Sonnets: Summer

THE FLYING CRUCIFIX

The Crystal Beach boys plied their bag of tricks.
The August sun which left their shoulders burned
Inspired the daring high-board leap they learned
And later named "The Flying Crucifix."

To start, they never stepped but ran to lunge
With arms outstretched removing east from west;
They hung and crossed their feet, as though for rest,
Suspending air and time before the plunge.

In quick descent they followed speed; their hair
And skin licked by the wind; from board to blue
Abyss the tingling backbones fell—then flew
In buoyant bodies up to light and air.

The reckless boys have found the shameless loss
And fearful thrill of taking up the cross.

Baptismal Leap

Earlier versions of the four poems comprising Seasoned Sonnets appeared in Bridges, Carl, ed. Jesus, God's Last Word: Essays in Honor of David L. Eubanks. *Knoxville: Tennessee Valley, 2004. Used by permission.*

Seasoned Sonnets: Autumn

HALLOWEEN

When all the world grows dark with fog and mist,
And through the tangled trees the vapors climb
Like winding, ghostly slugs whose strings of slime
Persist long after their nocturnal tryst—
And when those vapors float into the air
Like bony fingers, scratching deep the round,
Red, Jack-o-lantern moon, to drag it down
From sky to wood into the leafless lair—

We seek the glow of kitchen chairs and hearth
Where steaming coffee, tea, or chocolate fills
Our skull-white cups, elixir light, to kill
The fear of night and spooks that rise from earth.
This warm commune redeems each Halloween,
By grace and peace, into All Hallow's Eve.

Eucharist Celebration

Seasoned Sonnets: Winter

POLARIS

One dark December night, she stood beneath
A punctured sky where pricks of light, among
The silent holes of heaven, bled and sung
A haunted tune; it floated like a wreath
Through chilly air—transparent, woven white—
To crown Polaris with her thoughts of thorns,
These double points of insoluble horns—
The transient breath, the eternal light.

The swirl within her head—to fall or dance—
Compelled her ask again the constant North,
Through drifting haloed mist, a third and fourth
Request to find her footing, take her stance.
Her shadowed soul among that host flung far
Could only wait the Bright and Morning Star.

Dark Night of the Soul

Seasoned Sonnets: Spring

TESTIMONY

I feared the cold command of Death, a strife
That slit my soul with cold serrated dread;
But Jesus since has come back from the dead—
I lead my days, a free-to-care-for life.

I feared the Crypt whose shadow wrapped, in gloom,
My linen heart and grimed its edges frayed;
But Jesus since has come back from the grave—
I garden ground that stretches past my tomb.

I feared the gavel's last resounding whack
To face a just and darkened Wrath unfurled;
But Jesus since has come to court this world—
His plea and Counsel will reverse the black.

I say: His rising and return sets free
The change that changes everything—and me.

Witness to Hope

REFLECTED GLORY

Exposed in April's paradox—a spring
Turned winter: Deep and cold, nor'easter white—
We trudged through foot-deep snow that quiet night
Like silent monks, in tandem, worshiping.

The moon came up and set the scene ablaze;
It sparkled through each limb of ebony,
And we beheld this gleaming ecstasy
Like holy lunatics struck dumb, half-crazed;

And far beyond our sight, an endless weave
Of pulsing, vital light came spinning threads
Upon the moon, the road, the trees, our heads—
A glory steeped and stepped on Easter's eve.

Our shadows danced by grace of moonlight's mass
And beckoned to the shining fields we passed.

To David B. Reynolds

GREENSLEEVES

The ground-burst beats a golden genesis
As vibrant nature pulses vernal green:
Azaleas, daffodils, and hyacinths—
These scattered sparks of throbbing solar sheen.

So April's bluster buffets businessmen;
Their neckties slap and sail like soaring kites—
Like soaring salmon flail and fight with fin
And tail to breach the airy current's bite.

The morning tears—as clear as squeegeed glass—
Have scraped the chill gray sky and cleansed the dead
Earth dry—reviving Winter's withered grass
Until it blooms in shades from pink to red.

Such righteous riot tips the Maker's hand,
Adorns the mind in greensleeves from the land.

THANKSGIVING

The day has ended; all the work sits scraped
And stacked around the kitchen sink and stove.
How long before we set the chairs? Who knows—
For now, we laugh at tedium escaped.

We laugh at withered jokes, for old time's sake,
Suspending grievances, at least today.
The aftermath we'll later wash away
With family stories, sudsy heat and ache.

Tomorrow comes, and soon enough the song
We made—from flawed designs and faulty plans—
Awaits the cupboard shelf like pots and pans.
We note the storage place—most likely wrong.

So let the days we labor, love, and live
Replenish good with grace and thanks to give.

THOSE TIMES

Those times when shackled moments drag the ball
And twisted chain (imprisoned nights) or speed
As fast as Christmas morning (fancy flights)
Or stand as still as death (a gravestone pall)—

Those places where the room constricts the noose
Or blows the walls to kingdom come (displays
The wound)—nowhere to hide, nowhere to run—
Or where it draws a blank (undone and loose)—

These crush the heart below a stony heap
Or leave it locust-swarming (all in need)
Or plunge it quick beneath the yelping squall
Into the empty, silent, crushing deep.

But still, by time and space prevails the choice—
A whispered word, a small immobile Voice.

1 Kings 19:9b–13

Storage Tubs for
Christ's Mass

A CELEBRANT'S PRAYER

This season, stewed in celebration, stirs
The heart and leaves us stuffed with empty joy—
A meal of consolation in a toy
Or treat, a gift or game—digestive slurs.
These holidays of hectic pace increase
A pressured push beyond the heart's consent,
Where quick we ever trudge the next event
Or visit—infinity plagued of peace.

Oh, Breath of Heaven, whisper now of Bread
And Wine—come fill the soul, make hunger cease;
Come raise these dusty bones from walking dead.
Come brood upon the depth of our decease—
We trip along the empty way we dread—
Come help us see the Hope of our release.

Communion Meditation

Christmas Quartet

WAITING FOR CHRISTMAS

Anticipating—waiting for the time
To pass, for all things pass and leave us change
And changed. The waiting helps us find a range
Of work and play, and yet we wait a sign.

Anticipating—holding hope that change
Will bring a blessèd thing into our lives,
A thing so blessed that we must count by fives,
Or fifties, gauging good as something strange.

Anticipating—birth and death—the size
Of things we try to hold with little hands;
So much of life flows past the palm like sands,
Our castles built and crumbled, truth and lies.

Then on this Christmas eve, as we await,
May we redeem the time as good and great.

Christmas Quartet

TO OPEN GIFTS

To open gifts beneath a Christmas pine,
An infant sits amazed by foil and bows,
By light and sparkle. Rows and rows and rows
Of blazing boxes baffle little minds.

But soon enough the child, impatient, finds
Each package holds almost the heart's desire;
Each empty promise flames a thirsty fire
And counts the cost of gifts in every whine.

Once baleful ghosts of glint and greed have passed,
We gauge the gift by wear, in how we use
The thing, appraise its value to amuse
Or benefit; we know it cannot last.

How long before these fallen wrappers lift—
Before we trust the Giver of all gifts?

Christmas Quartet

HOUSE OF BREAD

In homes across the globe this noisy night—
On tables set with fear or greed—we feast
Our famished souls with flesh from plant and beast
Yet hunger still for water, air, and light.

We spread ourselves until, too thin, we scrape
Across our toasted lives, consumed as much
As we consume; as dog eat dog in crunch
Of bones, we snap and snarl with no escape.

But still the joy of better fare, a piece
Of bread with savored salt, invites us all
To dine aware that what appears as small
And weak, can raise the loaf on which we feast.

The call to dine still stands when all is said:
"Come, taste at Bethlehem the House of Bread."

Christmas Quartet

GRACE FOR CHRISTMAS EVE

Our gracious Father, thank You; join us here
This season, bless our company and meal;
For You have made us Yours; You placed Your Seal
On lonely lives and hearts impaired by fear.
And not content to leave us bruised, You healed
Our deafness, whispered *Love*, that single Word,
To give enduring Peace; for having heard
You call, we have become both forged and steeled.
And not content to orphan us, You gave
Us comfort through the people we befriend,
And then a Comforter to make amends,
Transforming all attachments that we crave.
Transform this gathering unto these ends—
Make friends family, and family friends.

A GATHERING OF FOWLS

On *Twelve* extended limbs of holly sat
Eleven birds, whose feathers glistened black;
They watched *Ten* geese gainsay, with click and clack,
Nine ducks who let the taunts roll off their backs.
A chorus *Eight* of lowly whippoorwills
Lamented under *Seven* blue jays' shrill
Complaint. *Six* sparrows fell before their fill
As finches *Five* arrayed their golden bills.
Four falcons slowly floated rings above
Three nesting hens immobilized and numb,
While in an oak perched owls, a *Brace* in sum,
That scrutinized a *Solitary* dove.

But each to each must fly to revelry
Beneath the Partridge on a dogwood tree.

CATHEDRAL EVE

The stones in sheer communion sit atop
Each other, colored here and there throughout
With flickered flame and held in place by grout
Of fellowship—they wait the Spirit's drop.

Across the mountains, deserts, oceans, streams,
Across the woods and lakes, the gulfs and plains,
Creation holds remembrance for the strains
Of angel song that filled the night with dreams.

So here we set—oh yes, we sense it—placed
By Purpose—dialectic'ly unsolved
While heaven hums a lyric unresolved
And whispers, "Look beyond this land of waste."

Just on the eve of this cathedral thresh,
We wait our reconstruction into Flesh.

1 Peter 2:5; Psalm 19:1

An Altered Advent

FIRST SUNDAY

"A glass of brandy neat"

Old Sweeney sits on padded pew, the next
To last, and contemplates the Sunday meal
With hope—no reason for becoming vexed
Communing with potatoes, carrots, veal.

If cosmic cataclysms crack his head
And draw his thought away from savory flesh,
He lifts his pudgy nose with lapsing dread
And sniffs the pine limbs scattered round the crèche.

And should a catastrophic sky descend
And all the stars and all the moons explode,
Old Sweeney knows just how the story ends—
No need to let the appetite implode.

For are we not all destined to attend
The wedding feast of Lamb—as guests and friends?

Hope

—Sweeney Erect

An Altered Advent

SECOND SUNDAY

"A wicked deck of cards"

She always enters fashionably late
And flows with stately semblance down the aisle—
Her head erect, her shoulders set, her smile
A Mona Lisa smile—Sly? Smug? Bent? Straight?

She settles in—pew six from front, the left
Hand side—and like a moth draws to a flame,
She draws her Tarot deck, denying shame,
From out her purse and plots her cosmic theft.

Between the death by water and the death
By flame, she calculates foretelling faith
To lay out one's impending, troubled wraith
And so reveal its last enshrouded breath.

Yes, Ms. Sosostris sees ahead and shows
The secret things not even Jesus knows.

Faith

>   —I. *The Burial of the Dead, The Wasteland*

An Altered Advent

THIRD SUNDAY

"A cat in profound meditation"

No one can see the vicar's cat remote
Inside the manger—slyly curled. Despite
Attempts to bar him hence, the furry fright,
In black and white, purrs praises from the throat.
If one could witness through Tuxedo's eye
And peer without a blink on rapture's fire,
Could one return to simple things—aspire
Again to cream and yarn and moonlit sky?

Or have the nine lives lived already bought
Their shadowed pleasure from desire of mice
And mates, of birds and snakes, of scoop and slice—
All manner of design, pursued and caught—
Until he lies slit-eyed in glad repose
To contemplate the name *he* only knows.

Joy

—Old Possum's Book of Practical Cats

An Altered Advent

FOURTH SUNDAY

"Do I dare?"

"I do not think you understand the face
It takes to mask the apprehending wound—
An overwhelming question, blue perfumed,
That sends us seeking even fractured grace.

"So let us go then, you and I, across
The town where piercing spires harpoon the holes
Of vaulted heaven, where unsettled souls
Can drown or burn away in fear of loss.

"For fear disturbed the days and nights we spent
In foggy, yellow talk imbrued—imbued—
And now in silence on this advent pew
We sit in-curled by winter's discontent.

"Unsettled—yes; perhaps at last I see
My need—anesthetized tranquility."

Peace

—The Love Song of J. Alfred Prufrock

CAROL

As if by winter's darkened spell of time,
The rich—and would-be—climb to deck their halls
Before they bustle off to shop the malls
And plow through flurried drifts of season's rhyme.

Exhausted by the fruitcake pace, they claim:
"Angels, we have heard, get high, smoking tokes
Of Mary Jane"—self-medicating jokes
In amber spirits, numbing out the pain.

Then as the household drifts uneasily
To sleep, they float a minor-keyed refrain:
"O, silent night, lonely night"—how insane
To celebrate our joy insistently.

O come, ye monied, dosing, emptied elves
And sing the manger song—Immanuel.

Table Crumbs for
Friends and Lovers

COLOR LINE

How could we know the blood upon our hands?
Our first-grade life obscured the ancient bane:
We learned our letters reading *Dick and Jane*,
And galloped free—no stocks, no bonds, no lands.

I did not know your color came from Old
Americans—the ones whose gods exchanged
Ancestral blood for *Mam* and maize—deranged
At last by Latin lust to lords and gold.

I did not know my color line cut through
The Old North World—where folk of fay encased
Their sacred prey in boggy peat—embraced
The wintered world by slashing throats askew.

How odd—your fathers left your skin blood-stained
While thirsty mother earth left mine blood-drained.

To Felipe (*Friend of Horses*)

Brownsville, Texas

Mam [măm]: A pan-Mayan kinship term for "Grandfather" or "grandson," as well as a term of respect referring to ancestors and deities.

YOKEFELLOW

That evening, long ago, you took my call,
An invitation that I made to dine,
And so began the decades' link—divine
Devotion's lean, like Barnabas and Saul.

For Sharon's Rose we undertook the field—
You labored by applying boardroom skill;
I plied consensus with a classroom will—
Transforming service to a sacred yield.

From valleys West and North of Tennessee
We brought our mates and found the shadows where
The slow decline and quick demise ensnare.
And still, I stand by you, and you by me—

In worship, work, and wives, we strain the steep;
We lean together, joyful as we weep.

To Bo Boaz

The Warren Trilogy

CADE'S COVE '97

November tumbles down the mountainside
And flows throughout the Cove this All Saints' Day
Where four companions risk the haunting gray
Of floating mists and halt their pilgrim's ride
To seek that orange spirit in the trees—
Concealed by streaks of red and streams of gold—
Until immersing rains retire them, cold
And damp, to rest beneath loquacious leaves.

Despite the soggy shoes and dripping hair,
A warmer laughter ripples limbs and grass—
A moment, lifted, like the sacred mass,
Transformed and pure as autumn's baptized air.
A day this good, with friends this good, inspires—
With spirit holy—friendship's tongue of fires.

To Joe and Jill

When the rains surprise

The Warren Trilogy

AROUND THE WORLD

Necessity may mother inventions,
But boredom fathers creative edges.
Unending days drove our competitions—
Indoors, in streets, across lawns and hedges.

We sped and sprang; we jounced and jumped; we skipped
The rules, until our egos shone like brass,
Since all relied on saving—face; we flipped
The fields contending hard for skill and class.

This afternoon, years past our boredom rite,
We shot away at 'Round the World; we claimed
The joy of mounting risk and mental psych;
Companionship leaves summer egos tamed.

I lost at World, but gained a soulful end—
Re-vision from a necessary friend.

To Joe

For sunny diversions

The Warren Trilogy

DEPARTURE

While speeding east, the rainless cover broke,
Unveiling, in October's closing light,
A pumpkin fireball paused in western flight;
It cloaked the forest hills in withy smoke.
A yellow poplar blaze, a maple spark
Of rouge, an ember's undergrowth in rust
Inflamed another year to crackling dust;
The ashes left a strange, familiar dark.

We trench the years against a gloomy light,
To spark the moments from our dimming past;
The firebreak that these visits form may last
The glowing day, but not expiring night.
The sojourn burnt with such long-standing friends
Rekindles heart—until the mem'ry ends.

To Joe

When the clouds roll in

IN PRAISE OF KNOWLEDGE, ENTHUSIASM, AND ENGAGEMENT

Of course the course objectives fit and fix
The institution's purposed goal. They ping
Locations—time and space—for Malcolm X,
Our Johnson U, and Martin Luther King.

With ease of laughter, dancing eyes, and bold
Wholeheartedness, she moves the text from page
To air—exuberance to turn and fold
The Black Arts Movement: Beauty, plea, and rage.

But practiced mind gives way to heart's desire—
To help reveal another's point of view;
And in that hope ignite a holy fire
To reconcile this schismed world anew.

Despite the time or silent students—fie—
Her teaching stirs come hell or water high.

Classroom Observation of April Conley Kilinski

African American Literature

LOVE KINDLED

A love impassioned—fire of white-hot flame—
Explodes the mind with searing flash and flush.
It strikes the heart in driving sheets of lust
To leave its lover blinded, scorched, and lame.

A love domestic—flame of sapphire heat—
Erects a picket fence to keep the good
Exchange of growing sparks, in brick and wood,
Within exclusive bounds where lovers meet.

But love communal—radiating gold—
Embraces all the hurt and hungry lost.
This open bonfire reckons worth, not cost,
Extending welcome from the vagrant cold.

All loves we kindle have their shining light,
But which among them stays the damning night?

For Josh Boaz

YOUR HEART OR MINE?

You've heard the joke regarding love and sex?
"She needs a reason; he just needs a place."
Between a *why* and *where* the passions race,
Yet we evade the end of torrid wrecks.

Can *why* meet *where*—engage a friendly brunch—
Without the wanton wreckage known to kill
The human soul, when bodies heat and spill
Like coffee at a Cracker Barrel lunch?

You've never said your *why*—the why you gave
Me passage back into your life and times;
I keep my *where* a paper chase—these rimes—
Each passing trip inscribe, each moment save.

The Way between your heart and mine I vow,
To have and hold forever, Love, and now.

THE BIRDS, THE BEES, THE MOON

It bears the shared consent of taking in
And slipping out—the hunted nest and bird
Where soothing agitation builds absurd
Relief from feathered joy and cracked chagrin.

Its words fly to and from, in and out—
Selective, salacious, seductive bees
Between the flower work and hive of ease,
Intent to ply and pulse the honey route.

A rising, cyclic rhythm, sure and set,
It pauses at the apex—moon at peak,
Suspended on a dark but shimmered sheet—
And then contracts to earth, cooled and wet.

The furnace flames in loving clemency—
This lifting breath and dust of ecstasy.

As the Song of Songs

CANDLE LIGHTING

By candle glow these lovers make their prayer
And pledge themselves to live a life most well.
The darkness of this evening they dispel,
Yet every hope and joy will have its care.

The flames of marriage burn not lightly, since
A kindling blood ignites their passions white;
Desire creates the force that fashions tight
One life of two—and more than two forth hence.

But marriage flames may burn as well as warm—
The fire may mar before its heat refines—
So as they reach to call each other "Mine,"
They know: "The Phoenix *blazes* as it's born."

In future days of heat and ash and blight,
Let marriage flames hold guard against the night.

For Ross and Ellen

HOPE

The candle flame glares hard, until a puff
Of air dissolves the blade into a plume
Of seaweed shadows, crashing through the room—
Her angry breath expelling with a huff.
She stops, leans in, and blows the stream away.
The fluid wax floods up the failing wick
Which fades—canary, amber, rust—a sick
Decay as curling smoke turns calloused clay.

The passing glow imprints his swirling mind.
Immobile, phantom memories inlay
The scene's relief—in black and white and gray—
Before the ghosted image leaves him blind.
But still, he reaches out at hope's demand,
Across the table, for her hazy hand.

LOVE'S LONG SHADOW

"You always hurt the one you love, the one
You shouldn't hurt at all"—and thus the strife
Of love's long shadow slits the bond of wife
And husband leaving senses dim and dumb.
Such silence blackens thoughts of sacrifice—
Eclipsing mercy, shoving peace aside—
Until the spectral thoughts possessed by Pride
Afflict us—frigid fire and burning ice.

So should we yield ourselves to grasping grief
And leave this home, turned house, an empty shell?
Or should we rage in this chaotic hell
To never know a moment's blessed relief?
Or can we strive to lift the marriage plight
By shielding one another in the fight?

―――――――――

"You always hurt the one you love . . .": Lyric by Doris Fisher & Allan Roberts

Plot Numbers for
Madison Cemeteries:
Grave Stories

HEADSTONES

*Like the old monarch's hand, this collection
"smells of mortality."*

—King Lear

*The death of a near acquaintance aroused . . .
in all who heard it the complacent feeling that,
"It is he who is dead and not I."*

—Leo Tolstoy

*The thing that hath been, it is that which shall be;
and that which is done is that which shall be done:
and there is no new thing under the sun.*

—Qoheleth

King Lear (4.6.133)

Leo Tolstoy, The Death of Ivan Ilyich *(1886), trans. Louise and Aylmer Maude; accessed June 19, 2020, https://www.lonestar.edu/departments/english/Tolstoy_Ivan.pdf.*

Ecclesiastes 1:9, King James Version (adapted).

MADISON CEMETERIES

Across these grounds, on phantom names I gaze
In rows made reverend by water, prayer,
And word; where Autumn sweeps the slumber bare;
Where children seldom play, nor cattle graze—
An empty space, except for grass and names
Imprinting stone and earth; but all soon fades
And fails to resurrect these scant remains:
The passing toils of men and strains of maids.
These names without their portraits, faceless words,
Lament and moan—forgotten breath and skin
Like fading grass that withers from within—
The saddest loss, like some forgotten bird
The flock has left to autumn's frosty breath:
This still-of-life becoming stiller death.

Benediction

Springdale Cemetery

JASON RITTER CROSLEY

1ST Lieut. Aviation Corps
World War of 1917 & 1918

In France, his riddled plane survived touchdown;
The Sopwith's engine belched blue smoke then died.
The maimed American surged from the side
And slid the wing—from cockpit to the ground.

He staggered twenty yards and swayed before
The fresh, mown hay rose up—a guarding flood.
His shattered right arm, his boots filled with blood,
Left senses numb but made the body sore.

He rolled on his back in a gloaming daze,
Recalled a sky—September—just the same
As that above—a high-school football game—
He walked her home through fading aqua haze.

Of all he wished to see below these skies,
He most desired her dancing, azure eyes.

Fallen

Springdale Cemetery

SON

in loving memory

CONNOR ADLER CARR

April 9, 1954
July 20, 1978

He could not fill the void of ending loss;
Divorce now left him weaving countless cost
Of what to keep, to yield, to leave, to toss—
Till every knotted nerve grew numb with frost.

That chilling stab, the crystalline despair,
Diffused his will with ever-freezing grasp
Until his eyes became a vacant stare,
A weary gray from heartless woman's blast.

Paralysis of thought—the very dead
Of winter—stands a trembling cattail stalk
On barren bands. No longer could he talk;
No longer would he twist the words she said.

He grieved his emptied soul with loss of hope
And left the grief at the end of a rope.

Binding Pain

Springdale Cemetery

Roxy Brook

BUTLER

1927—1958

A rain so gentle—she could almost count
Each April tear that touched her upturned face
As clouds, chrome-blunted, checked their hectic race.
She watched the shifting shapes collide and mount
Above her glazing eyes. She thought she saw
The manes of horses sweeping down the sky—
The heads of four oncoming horses fly
With foaming lips, their nostrils red and raw.

Above the scene, a red and garish trace
Reflected round and round in hanging mist.
The ambulance, lopsided, off the curve,
Awaited cargo broken by the swerve
Of skidding tires—sharp turn, wet road kissed.
The clouds could count each blood-drop on her face.

Horsepower

Springdale Cemetery

WALTER SANDS

Jan. 29, 1855
June 22, 1920.

Some silence swirling in the snow refused
To let him speak of love. They walked ahead—
His hand upon her glove—her cheeks flushed red;
His heart half dead—rejection's pounding bruise.

They walked while silence drifted higher up
The road, their boots, their souls—until at last
The ring she gave him back slipped through his grasp
And left his shriveled ego drawn and cut.

Then something in the swirling snow recalled
Her voice—a muffled air with piercing cold—
As step by step they trudged beside an old
Dilapidated fence, exposed and bald.

She said, "I don't believe in wasting breath."
Nor will you, thought he, *in your lonely death.*

Silence Swirling

Springdale Cemetery

MATILDA A. SANDS

Feb. 4, 1855
Feb. 9, 1920

"Come sit with me a moment longer. Tell
Me of your day. The night approaches fast
At hand, and soon my feet must walk the last
Uncluttered way to heaven—or to hell.

"I see the darkness by amazing light,
A clarity that murky dullness pricks
In ways that only those in lost and sick
Conditions may—the kiss of lonely night.

"So kiss me, now, with wintered lips inflamed
By something silent in the snow—we dared
Not speak a passion that we never shared
But kept our souls serene, secure, and tamed.

"Remember, when the snow enshrouds my rest,
The second bed you shared has proved the best."

Second Best

Madison State Hospital Cemetery

MALINDA P. CORT
*1858 * 1934*

A windy river through the trees gives voice
To all the dying leaves who sing the dirge
Of autumn's falling, failing, fatal urge
To hold its shade and hue by force of choice.

But something, like a silence in the snow,
Cannot withstand abuse of wasting breath—
Cannot refuse the airy song of death—
The thought of passion drifting long ago.

She shuts her bedroom window tight against
The noisy night's proposal—wild and fierce;
She puts to bed the head and heart that pierce
Her soul—a bald, dilapidated fence.

By morning's light, in need of tub and rake,
The voices lie—but hers will not awake.

Autumn Voices

Madison State Hospital Cemetery

D. S.

939

On summer nights, she sat beside the woods
Behind the house where ceaseless voices slid—
The crickets, cicadas, and katydids—
Into her thoughts of disappointed *shoulds*.

Her agitation grew, and by that brink
She listened to the dreadful facts of life,
And then she took to sheltering a knife.
He found her, half bled out, beside the sink.

His visits grew as distant as her stare—
Refused to see him winter, spring, then fall—
Until one year he did not come at all.
She never knew he abandoned her there.

No longer speak those ceaseless voices low;
She has her quiet in this pauper's row.

Voices

Madison State Hospital Cemetery

L. R.

124

By evening's gray, she searches all the bluff
Engulfed in shadows ever deepening—
She cannot hear the clatter or the ring
From barges docking in the river's sluff.

Little Boy Blue, what will you do? she moans.
*When the wind blows, where do you go? Where do
You go, when the wind blows? What will you do,
Little Boy—?* Her churning memory roams

Among the bending oaks as autumn's wind
Beguiles the trees to creak, to crack, to groan
And blows away the frantic yells from home.
Then like the troubled trunks, her shoulders bend.

She asks; she seeks; she knocks without relief
And wanders—serpentine—the copse of grief.

Wanderer

St. Joseph's Cemetery

BASS

Carel
1867 * 1912

A distant wail, collapsing from the sky,
Engulfs the fallen man amid the hay.
He sees the pulsing grass—hypnotic—sway
Like passing boxcars, rock-and-rolling by.

The thrumming, drumming in his head recalled
A rhythmic, locomotive pull that fades
Beneath descending cliffs along the grade's
Dark narrows—carbon stung and cinder galled.

The weight within his chest expands to crush
The thickened air that clogs his lungs. It thumps
Like massive wheels on rails—pa pump, pa pump—
Then stutters like wings of a startled thrush.

Next, all grows still, and light begins to fail;
Yet, somewhere off, he hears a distant wail.

Wail

St. Joseph's Cemetery

GEROD TELEK, JR.

Dec. 23, 1864
May 1, 1925

The dingy window faced a northern view.
On bright days, gloomy shades infused the look;
On cloudy ones, a shadow edged the nook
With blackened spiderwebs that fell askew.
A mortared, yellow wall with cracks like thread
Obscured the heart of ever seeing grass
Again, as if the grimed, arachnid glass
Could hope to hide this secret killing bed.

So day upon eternal day he spied
Into the webbed abyss—his memory
As dark and bricked as any endless hole—
A bottled, breaded, bathed forgotten fly,
Awaiting angels—dark and cloaked—to free
His warehoused, trapped, and inventoried soul.

Svidrigailov's Hell

Bayless Cemetery

ILLEGIBLE INSCRIPTION

In dim October light, the Weather heaps
A cloudy harvest overhead and reaps
The rain with crooked scythe that forks and leaps
From cloud to cloud; from cloud to earth It weeps
A tortured streaming, beating down a deep
Tormented sigh of rising winds that creep
And crack in restive limbs where gravestones keep
The fatal secrets bound to mortal sleep.

But secrets have a way of slipping piece
By piece from chiseled groove and lettered lease;
The viscous howl and splattered fist release
Small flecks of stones—memorial's decrease.
Thus trust and dreams and all affections cease
Beneath the rain's erasure—"R st n P c "

Weathered

NOTES ON THE CEMETERIES

Springdale Cemetery

Springdale Cemetery became Madison's third burial site circa 1839.

The small village of Fulton, adjoining Madison on the southeast end along the Ohio River, had the area's first cemetery.

During a flood in the late 1880s, some of the bodies in Madison's second burial site, the Old Third Street Cemetery, washed away. Thereafter, residents ceased to use that location as a burial site, later moving the surviving stones to higher ground at the Fairmount Cemetery (on Michigan Road, North Madison) and to the Springdale Cemetery, located on the north side of Crooked Creek.

These events left Springdale the only surviving cemetery located in the downtown area of Madison.

Madison State Hospital Cemetery

Only seventeen tombstones, plus one funeral home marker, give the names of those buried here. Metal crosses with an etched plate of the person's initials and patient number mark the rest of the graves.

St. Joseph's Cemetery

Located on North Walnut Street, St. Joseph's Cemetery lies at the bottom of Hatcher Hill, next to the old glue factory site.

Bayless Cemetery

The Bayless Cemetery began as a family cemetery on the farm of Nathaniel and Mary Bayless, on Paper Mill Road, near Wirt.

www.ingramcontent.com/pod-product-compliance
Lightning Source LLC
Chambersburg PA
CBHW061509040426
42450CB00008B/1531